Route 321

Route 321: **On Communion**

BY
Jonathan Feathers

RESOURCE *Publications* · Eugene, Oregon

ROUTE 321
On Communion

Resource Publications
An Imprint of Wipf and Stock Publishers
199 W. 8th Ave., Suite 3
Eugene, OR 97401

www.wipfandstock.com

PAPERBACK ISBN: 979-8-3852-2639-9
HARDCOVER ISBN: 979-8-3852-2640-5
EBOOK ISBN: 979-8-3852-2641-2

VERSION NUMBER 02/21/25

To Melanie, Dorothy, J.W. and all who have encouraged me in ministry.

I meditate on your precepts and consider your ways.

Psalm 119:15 NIV

Contents

Part II: New Testament

Introduction

Meditate

Route 321: On Communion consists of 66 communion meditations, from selected passages of Scripture, one from each book of the Bible. Each communion meditation has a title, followed by a verse of Scripture, a communion meditation, and space for journaling. The 321 framework serves as a guide for each meditation. The 321 framework is listed below to guide you using this resource either privately or for preparing your own communion meditation. Here are some suggestions on approaching each meditation:

- Take 3 minutes to read the meditation
- Take 2 minutes to pray and reflect upon the meditation
- Take 1 minute to respond to the meditation in the additional space on the page

As you read and reflect upon each thought, feel inspired to record a response. You may even write your own communion meditation based upon the same verse of Scripture. If so, here is how you may respond or begin to write your own communion meditation by using the following questions:

Question 1: What is one word, or phrase, from the Bible that captures your attention?

Question 2: How does this word capture
the audience's attention?

Question 3: How does this scripture or word prepare
the audience for communion?

These three questions may prove helpful for you. If you would like to learn more, then the appendix includes a step-by-step process in developing a communion meditation. Furthermore, *Route 321: On Communion* serves as a resource for your devotion to Christ. Feel free to use this resource privately, to be read aloud as a communion meditation, or to inspire you to develop a communion meditation, within your church.

Part I: **Old Testament**

Chapter 1

Speech

"Now the whole world had one language
and a common speech."

GENESIS 11:1

AFTER GOD CREATED THE heavens and the earth, everyone spoke the same language. Everyone understood each other for there was one common language. The Bible indicates there were not multiple languages or speeches until the tower of Babel. Think of the endless potential and possibilities that could exist today if there were not language barriers. Communication would flow much smoother.

When Jesus walked the earth, hundreds of languages existed. Just before Jesus' arrest, crucifixion, and resurrection, he instituted the Lord's Supper, also known as communion in some traditions. The two emblems of bread and juice can and have brought Christians back to a common language. Communion communicates the remembrance of what Jesus did and how he conquered the grave. Today, Christians have a common language through communion that directs us to Jesus.

Chapter 2

Song

"The Lord is my strength and my song; he has become my salvation. He is my God, and I will praise him, my father's God, and I will exalt him."

EXODUS 15:2

SONGS. I BELIEVE MOST, if not all, of us have songs that we really enjoy. When we feel sad, we listen to a song. When we feel happy, we listen to a song. When we feel one way, but prefer to feel another, we listen to a song. If we do not know a song, we may even make one up.

A song was sung after the Israelites crossed the red sea. This song acknowledged the strength of the Lord and his deliverance from oppressors. We should sing a similar song acknowledging our deliverance from sin, the salvation that is available to us through Jesus.

Chapter 3

Atonement

"This is to be a lasting ordinance for you: Atonement is
to be made once a year for all the sins of the Israelites."

LEVITICUS 16:34A

ATONEMENT—A WORD WE DO not often use in our English language every day. Atonement carries numerous meanings for it may
include mercy, justice, and grace. The Israelites were commanded
to observe a day of atonement for the sins of the people. At communion, we remember Jesus was offered as a sacrifice for the sins
of all people for all of time. Through Jesus, we are offered mercy,
justice, and grace.

Chapter 4

Acknowledged

"Now Moses was a very humble man, more humble
than anyone else on the face of the earth."

NUMBERS 12:3

WHEN I READ THESE words, I respect the description of Moses. To
be mentioned is one thing, but to be acknowledged for character
is something else. Moses experienced the work of God, through
the plagues, the crossing of the Red Sea, and the provisions in
the wilderness. Moses revered God and gave God the respect
that only God deserves. As Moses humbled himself before an al-
mighty God, we should remember the incredible act of what God
did for us by sending Jesus to die on the cross for our sins. We too
should revere God and His Glory.

Chapter 5

Forget

"Be careful that you do not forget the Lord your God"

DEUTERONOMY 8:11

FORGET. THERE ARE SOME memories we love to remember, while there are some we would love to forget. There are some we can remember as if we were still living in that moment remembering the sights, sounds, and smells, everything our senses would reveal to us. However, as humans, we forget. Therefore, we need reminders. Communion is a wonderful opportunity to remember Jesus' crucifixion, so that we do not forget His sacrifice or of God's love for us.

Chapter 6

Choose

"But as for me and my household,
we will serve the Lord."

JOSHUA 24:15B

"NOW FEAR THE LORD and serve him with all faithfulness. Throw away the gods your forefathers worshiped beyond the River and in Egypt, and serve the Lord. But if serving the Lord seems undesirable to you, then choose for yourselves this day whom you will serve...But as for me and my household, we will serve the Lord" says Joshua 24:14-15 These words from Joshua remind us at communion to choose who we worship. Do we worship something else or the God who loves us by sending his son Jesus to live, die, and rise again?

Chapter 7

Tent Peg

"But Jael, Heber's wife, picked up a tent peg and a
hammer and went quietly to him while he lay fast
asleep, exhausted. She drove the peg through his
temple into the ground, and he died."

JUDGES 4:21

HAVE YOU EVER DRIVEN a tent peg into the ground with a hammer? Consider the descriptive words in this verse. As grotesque as this seems, imagine what Jesus endured as the nails were driven into his hands and feet to the cross. Jesus was awake and aware of what was taking place unlike the man who was asleep. In His exhaustion, Jesus stayed the course, so that we could be reunited with Him.

Chapter 8

Foreigner

"At this, she bowed down with her face to the ground.
She exclaimed, "Why have I found such favor in your
eyes that you notice me—a foreigner?"

RUTH 2:10

HAVE YOU EVER FELT like a stranger in a foreign land? You have
experienced being out of your native country. You may not speak
the language, and everything seems a little different. Often at that
moment, travelers begin to be thankful for their homeland. Ruth
was found with favor as a foreigner in a strange land. As sinners,
God notices us, yet He does not leave us as foreigners. God sent
Jesus to the cross, so that we could enter God's home through Jesus.

Chapter 9

Consider

"But be sure to fear the Lord and serve him faithfully with all your heart; consider what great things he has done for you."

1 SAMUEL 12:24

HOW OFTEN DO WE forget about what others have done for us? We forget about a friend who pays for a meal. We forget how much our parents may have sacrificed for us. We forget about those who have given their time for our protection and safety within our communities and nation. Just like the Israelites, we are prone to forget what God has done. Communion is an opportune time to stop and remember what God has done for us through Jesus rather than forget. So, let us consider God's love for us.

Chapter 10

Notice

"Mephibosheth bowed down and said, "What is your servant, that you should notice a dead dog like me?"

2 SAMUEL 9:8

THIS IS NOT YOUR typical communion meditation, but there is something here. Listen to Mephibosheth words in response to King David, "What is your servant, that you should notice a dead dog like me?" Mephibosheth felt like an outcast to the king and so did we. We feel like outcasts and rightly so because we have sinned against God. However, God notices us. In fact, God noticed and loved his creation so much that he was willing to send His Son Jesus to die on the cross, so that we could dine with Him at His table in His kingdom someday. Like Mephibosheth, the king notices us.

Chapter 11

Contain

"But will God really dwell on earth? The heavens, even the highest heaven, cannot contain you. How much less this temple I have built!"

1 KINGS 8:27

HAVE YOU EVER WALKED into a stadium either empty or filled? Consider Neyland stadium where the University of Tennessee Volunteers football games are played or the Bristol Motor Speedway. Both can seat thousands of people. As large as these stadiums are, they cannot contain God. The tomb would not contain the crucified Jesus. Because of Jesus, we can gain access to where God dwells.

Chapter 12

Whirlwind

"As they were walking along and talking together,
suddenly a chariot of fire and horses of fire appeared
and separated the two of them, and Elijah went up to
heaven in a whirlwind."

2 KINGS 2:11

I HAVE SEEN DUST devils; whirlwinds of dirt spinning in the des-
ert. Imagine the shock as this appeared and Elijah was taken into
Heaven. Jesus was also taken up as he was talking to his disciples.
After Jesus died on the cross and rose again, the Bible describes
Jesus' ascension heavenward. It is because of Jesus that we may be
able to join him someday.

Chapter 13

Articles

"Now devote your heart and soul to seeking the Lord your God. Begin to build the sanctuary of the Lord God, so that you may bring the ark of the covenant of the Lord and the sacred articles belonging to God into the temple that will be built for the Name of the Lord."

1 CHRONICLES 22:19

I WOULD VENTURE OUT to say that most people have sacred articles. We may not use that specific terminology or vocabulary, but we do possess sentimental items such as family heirlooms. We are sentimental in God's sight. He would do anything for us, and he did by sending Jesus to die on the cross so that we could be with him.

Chapter 14

Build

"The temple I am going to build will be great, because our God is greater than all other gods."

2 CHRONICLES 2:5

WHY DO WE LIKE to build? You can watch children build a tower out of blocks, a fort out of a blanket, or even a boat out of pillows. It seems building is engrained within us. God is in the construction business. However, no building can contain Him. It takes Jesus to build a bridge back to God, so that we can join Him in the place he is preparing for us.

Chapter 15

Devote

"For Ezra had devoted himself to the study and observance of the Law of the Lord, and to teaching its decrees and laws in Israel."

EZRA 7:10

WHAT IS YOUR PASSION? What do you enjoy doing with your time? I have seen mechanics spend their free time repairing cars. I have seen carpenters spend their free time carving. I have seen artists paint, musicians play, athletes practice because they are passionate. Ezra devoted himself to the Law of the Lord because he was passionate. God also has an interest—in you and me. In his love for us, God sent Jesus to the cross and to rise again.

Chapter 16

Stood

"Ezra opened the book. All the people could see him because he was standing above them; and as he opened it, the people all stood up."

Nehemiah 8:5

At dedicated events, we often stand as a sign of attention and respect. We acknowledge something significant is about to take place. While on the cross, people stood watching at what was happening to Jesus. If they were not standing, then they were on their knees. Either way, people acknowledge how great God is and what He has done for us through Jesus.

Chapter 17

Time

"And who knows but that you have come to royal
position for such a time as this?"

ESTHER 4:14B

TIMING IS CRITICAL. IF the timing is not right, then you may burn
the cake in the oven. If the timing is not right, then the paint may
not be dry. If you hesitate, then you may miss an opportunity.
God knows about timing. Esther seized the opportunity at the
right time for her people. God seized the right time to save his
people from their sins by sending Jesus.

Chapter 18

Prosperous

"After Job had prayed for his friends, the Lord made
him prosperous again and gave him twice as much
as he had before."

JOB 42:10

IF YOU KNOW ANYTHING about Job know this, he made Job. Much
had been taken from him, yet Job did not curse or blame God.
Eventually, Job blesses God even though Job lost his children, pos-
sessions, and part of his health. God created mankind. In the midst
of a sin-filled world, God provides a way to be prosperous through
Jesus. We may not enjoy the earthly blessings, but we can enjoy the
heavenly blessings because of Jesus' death and resurrection.

Chapter 19

Buy Back

"Defend my cause and redeem me; preserve my life
according to your promise."

PSALMS 119:154

YOU MAY RECALL, OR even experience, an automotive campaign to
stimulate economic growth by returning a used car, or clunker, for
credit towards the purchase of a better fuel-efficient vehicle. Hundreds of thousands of people took advantage of this opportunity.

Jesus paid the full price to redeem us from sin, from clunker-
filled lives, when He died on the cross. Unlike some financial cam-
paigns that ended, Jesus' offer remains to this day. Let us be ever
grateful for what God has done for us through His Son Jesus.

Chapter 20

Train

"Train a child in the way he should go, and when he
is old he will not turn from it."

PROVERBS 22:6

AS ADULTS, WE WONDER how we could train, or start, a child on
a God-honoring path in life. We are not alone. We get a small
glimpse into the life of Jesus at an early age from Luke 2:41-42
states "every year his parents went to Jerusalem for the Feast of
the Passover. When he was twelve years old, they went up to the
Feast, according to the custom." An example was set. According
to Luke 2, Jesus was obedient. Not only did Jesus obey his earthly
parents, but Jesus also obeyed His Heavenly Father by enduring
death on a cross and being raised to life.

Chapter 21

Good Name

"A good name is better than fine perfume, And the
day of death better than the day of birth."

ECCLESIASTES 7:1

DOROTHY, J.W., MELANIE, BILLY, Joseph; newfound parents, at
times, struggle with finding the right name for a child. Jesus' name
was selected, and his parents were informed when they discovered
the pregnancy. Jesus' name would serve a purpose for mankind.
Jesus not only died but arose three days later. At communion, let
us remember the name of Jesus and his significance.

Chapter 22

Your Love

"Let him kiss me with the kisses of his mouth
—for your love is more delightful than wine."

SONG OF SOLOMON 1:2

WHEN WE HEAR OR read these words, we often picture an infatuation or romantic relationship between two people. Have you ever considered God's love for his creation? What has God done to demonstrate His love for us? God loves us so much that he sent Jesus to be born, live, die, and rise again. Jesus came to restore God's creation with him. Jesus is the manifestation of God's love.

Chapter 23

Salvation

"Surely God is my salvation; I will trust and not be
afraid. The Lord, the Lord, is my strength and my
song; he has become my salvation." With joy you will
draw water from the wells of salvation."

ISAIAH 12:2-3

DURING THIS CHRISTMAS SEASON, where do you find joy? Joy
can be found wrapped in a manger in a baby named Jesus, whose
name means Jehovah is salvation. As Isaiah proclaimed, surely
God is my salvation. In this gift to us from God, we can trust and
not be afraid; we can find a source of strength; we can experience
joy because of what Jesus did for us by dying on the cross and
being brought back to life. Let us share the gift of joy, the gift of
salvation, the gift of Jesus.

Chapter 24

Knew

"The word of the Lord came to me, saying, "Before
I formed you in the womb I knew you, before you
were born I set you apart; I appointed you as a
prophet to the nations.""

JEREMIAH 1:4-5

As God knew Jeremiah, God knew about the coming birth of
Jesus. God sent angels to inform Joseph and Mary. God knew
Jesus would be born with a mission and purpose. Jesus stayed
the course being obedient to his heavenly Father. Jesus obeyed to
the point of death on a cross and the resurrection from the tomb
to give us new life.

Chapter 25

Seek

"The Lord is good to those whose hope is in him,
to the one who seeks him."

LAMENTATIONS 3:25

HAVE YOU EVER PLAYED hide and go seek? My children love to play this game, most of the time they enjoy hiding underneath a blanket awaiting to be found. At discovery, they laugh and say let us hide again. In a way, we are hiding from God in sin. However, God does not leave us in the darkness alone. He finds us. He finds us through Jesus, who came to this earth to die on the cross and rise from the tomb. His sacrifice brings light, so that our sins can be removed, and we can be with Him.

Chapter 26

Sheep

"You my sheep, the sheep of my pasture are people,
and I am your God, declares the Sovereign Lord."

EZEKIEL 34:31

BAA, THE SHEEP SAYS. Who, what, when, where, why, how, the person asks. Both are looking for guidance and direction. A shepherd knows his sheep; a shepherd knows his people. The shepherd will look out for his sheep. The good shepherd looks out for us. He wants to guide us and direct us; however, we find ourselves wandering away. We wandered so far away from God that he went to great lengths to bring us back. Jesus came so that we could hear the shepherd's voice and return.

Chapter 27

Dominion

"He was given authority, glory and sovereign power;
all peoples, nations and men of every language worshiped him. His dominion is an everlasting dominion that will not pass away, and his kingdom is one
that will never be destroyed."

DANIEL 7:14

AS THIS WAS RECORDED in the book of Daniel, we understand who
this was referring to. This one given authority, who will be worshiped by all, and whose kingdom will never end is Jesus. Jesus died
on the cross and arose to be given this authority. May we remember
what Jesus went through and acknowledge him in his glory.

Chapter 28

Show

"Yet I will show love to the house of Judah; and I will save them—not by bow, sword or battle, or by horses and horsemen, but by the Lord their God."

HOSEA 1:7

HOW DO YOU SHOW love? Do you show love by saying it? Do you show love by giving someone something? Do you show love in some other way? God showed us love through Jesus. Jesus was born, lived, died, and lives again. God shows us love in Jesus not by bow or battle, but by sacrifice and service.

Chapter 29

Rend

"Rend your heart and not your garments. Return to
the Lord your God, for he is gracious and compas-
sionate, slow to anger and abounding in love, and he
relents from sending calamity."

JOEL 2:13

HAVE YOU EVER RETURNED an item to a department or retail
store? Maybe you were dissatisfied and wanted a full refund, or
you wanted to exchange it for a different item. God wants us to
turn to him. He wants our full heart focus not our lip service.
Through Jesus, God made an exchange that would remove our
sins, so that we could be with him.

Chapter 30

House

"This is what the Lord says to the house of Israel:
Seek me and live."

Amos 5:4

Houses, apartments, townhomes, however you might refer-
ence them, they are a dwelling place you refer to as home, a base
of operations for daily living cooking, cleaning, and sleeping. A
house is important to us. Jesus came to this earth in preparation
for a new home, one where God dwells. To gain access, Jesus would
need to die and rise again.

Chapter 31

Deliverer

"Deliverers will go up on Mount Zion to govern the mountains of Esau. And the kingdom will be the Lord's."

OBADIAH 21

I LIKE DELIVERIES, ESPECIALLY when something is ordered. Sometimes we often overlook the deliverer. The deliverer is important because if not for that person there would be no delivery. For us to be reconciled to God, there had to be a deliverer. In this case, the delivery is also the deliverer, which is Jesus. Jesus is the gift and the means of the gift. It is by Jesus that we are reconciled to God and by how we can enter God's kingdom.

Chapter 32

Inside

"But the Lord provided a great fish to swallow Jonah, and Jonah was inside the fish three days and three nights."

JONAH 1:17

JONAH IS A REMARKABLE story. Inside this fish, Jonah stayed. Imagine what Jonah encountered, nothing but complete darkness. Imagine what Jonah heard, the groans of this great fish and the rushing of water. Imagine what Jonah smelled, the remains of other fish. Try to imagine. Jesus referenced Jonah being in the great fish for three days in comparison to what he would face. Jesus was placed in a tomb, dark, silent, and empty. Like Jonah, Jesus did not remain. Jonah was spit out, while Jesus arose.

Chapter 33

Wait

"But as for me, I watch in hope for the Lord, I wait
for God my Savior; my God will hear me."

MICAH 7:7

HAVE YOU WAITED IN anticipation for your name to be called?
Take a doctor's office for instance. You wait at the doctor's office
because you are sick. You wait and wait for your name to be called
because once your name is called, you are one step closer to a diag-
nosis as to why you are sick and a step closer to getting treatment.
For years, people cried out to God for deliverance, and they did
not know what was wrong. At just the right time, God responded
by diagnosing sin and providing a cure—Jesus.

Chapter 34

Refuge

"The Lord is good, a refuge in times of trouble.
He cares for those who trust in him"

NAHUM 1:7

HAVE YOU EVER NEEDED a safe place, security, or protection from
the weather? You would need shelter, sun protection, sunscreen,
and a defense mechanism. Where would you turn for protection
from times of trouble? God can provide protection. From sin, God
provides protection through Jesus. Jesus' death on the cross and
subsequent resurrection from the dead provides a protection from
the consequences of sin. God cares for us.

Chapter 35

Waters

"For the earth will be filled with the knowledge of
the glory of the Lord, as the waters cover the sea."

HABAKKUK 2:14

O TO COUNT THE droplets of water in a raindrop, in a glass, in a
tub, in a pool, or in an ocean. Consider the number of droplets it
takes to fill a glass, much less an ocean. Like the number of water
droplets, the glory of the Lord is immeasurable. God's glory does
not begin nor end with water but extends to a demonstration of his
love to us by sending Jesus to die and live again.

Chapter 36

Mighty

"The Lord your God is with you, he is mighty to save. He will take great delight in you, he will quiet you with his love, he will rejoice over you with singing."

ZEPHANIAH 3:17

GOD IS MIGHTY. IN Jesus' mighty act upon the cross, we fall silent before this act of God's great love for us. Jesus' death demonstrates that God will go to mighty lengths to save us. At communion, let us be silenced by his love and rejoice with his might.

Chapter 37

I am with you

"Then Haggai, the Lord's messenger, gave this message of
the Lord to the people: I am with you, declares the Lord."

HAGGAI 2:13

ISN'T IT REASSURING TO hear certain words repeated on a consistent basis? For instance, "I love you," words you may have heard or even spoken; the consistency of these words reassures us, comforts us. The Lord declared, "I am with you" to Abraham, to Joshua, to Jeremiah; yes—Jesus also spoke these same words to his disciples and even to His Church. Through communion, we remember what Jesus did for us and that His Spirit is with us. I echo those some words for you again today—"I am with you, declares the Lord."

Chapter 38

Garments

"Then he said to Joshua, "See, I have taken away your
sin, and I will put rich garments on you."

ZECHARIAH 3:4A

DOES ANYONE LIKE DOING laundry? I could be wrong, but it is
never ending. As soon as one load of laundry is complete, it is time
to start another whether it is linens or delicate items. Each piece
of material gets dirty and needs to be cleaned. We, too, are dirty
and sinned stained. However, God does not leave us that way. Jesus came so that we could be forgiven, and our sins washed away.
Because of Jesus we can put on new garments.

Chapter 39

Awe

"My covenant was with him, a covenant of life and peace, and I gave them to him; this called for reverence and he revered me and stood in awe of my name."

MALACHI 2:5

A COVENANT, OR PROMISE, involves two parties, much like a contract. If both parties uphold their respective agreements, then all is well. When one party breaches the contract, trouble ensues. Mankind turned from God by sinning. With sin, there is separation from God. However, God does not leave it this way. Jesus came so a bridge could be built, and mankind no longer be separated from God and because of God's love for us, we revere him.

Part II: **New Testament**

Chapter 40

Proclamation

"She will give birth to a son, and you are to
give him the name Jesus, because he will save
his people from their sins."

Matthew 1:21

In silence, complete and utter silence, comes the rushing cries of a newborn baby boy; a baby boy born on a beautiful night bringing forth new hope, new faith, and new life. A night an angel once declared: She will give birth to a son and be named Jesus, because he will save his people from their sins.

This was more than just a few words; it was a proclamation, a proclamation not like any before or after his birth, a proclamation initiated by God, for Jesus would live, die, and rise back to life, so that we could experience a new life. At communion, we remember that Jesus saves us from our sins and offers us new life through him, for him and in him.

Chapter 41

His Baptism

"You are my Son, whom I love; with you
I am well pleased."

MARK 1:11B

AT THE BEGINNING OF his earthly ministry, the gospel of Mark records "Jesus came from Nazareth in Galilee and was baptized by John in the Jordan. As Jesus was coming up out of the water, he saw heaven being torn open and the Spirit descending on him like a dove. And a voice from heaven: You are my Son, whom I love; with you I am well pleased." At the end of his earthly ministry, the angel said, "Don't be alarmed. You are looking for Jesus the Nazarene, who was crucified. He has risen! He is not here. See the place where they laid him."

Between His baptism and His resurrection is the Cross—a defining moment for all humanity. At the Cross, we remember His earthly ministry. At the Cross we remember His body and His blood. At the Cross, Jesus is lifted above all. As we commune, let us lift Him up for what He did for us at the Cross.

Chapter 42

Be Ready

"You also must be ready, because the Son of Man
will come at an hour when you do not expect him."

LUKE 12:40

PICTURE THIS: YOU WALK into a restaurant, give the host your
name, and you receive a buzzer along with the instructions—the
wait is about 30 minutes. What do you do for the next 30 minutes?
Do you run a quick errand in hopes of returning before your table
is ready? You realize you must stay close by so that your buzzer will
alert you or listen for your name to be called to tell you your table
is ready. You do not want to miss out because that is the reason for
the wait. At communion, we remember Jesus has already paid the
bill through His death and resurrection; however, we also must be
ready when He returns or calls our name.

Chapter 43

Stress

"I have told you these things, so that in me you may
have peace. In this world you will have trouble. But
take heart! I have overcome the world."

JOHN 16:33

JESUS IS RIGHT YOU know, "in this world you will have trouble."
Trouble or stresses come in the form of many ways—health concerns, bills, time. Many of these may come to mind right now.
Then Jesus says, "But take heart! I have overcome the world."
Through the cross and tomb, Jesus brings victory! Jesus has overcome this world with all its troubles, its stresses. Repeat these
words after me, "In this world you will have trouble. But take
heart! I have overcome the world."

Chapter 44

Bread

"They devoted themselves to the apostles' teaching and to the fellowship, to the breaking of bread and to prayer."

ACTS 4:32

MANY MORNINGS MY GRANDMOTHER would wake up before sunrise and begin making bread, mixing the ingredients, placing them in a bowl and covering it while the dough rose. Then after several hours, my grandmother would continue the process of making homemade buttered rolls you could smell as she baked them in the oven. A simple piece of food it is—bread. We often consider bread a staple of our diet, the need for grain for the physical human body. Jesus uses a piece of bread to remind us of an incredible act that he would endure through his death on the cross and then his resurrection. Let us never forget Jesus instituted the bread which reminds us of his body and the juice his blood.

Chapter 45

Rejection

"Christ died for us."

ROMANS 5:8B

REJECTED. LIKE YOU, I have been rejected, turned down, or even turned away from something, whether it is a job opportunity, sports team, or something else. At times, we may even feel rejected by God. We can, however, overcome this fear of rejection. Romans 5:8 says, "But God demonstrates his own love for us in this: while we were still sinners, Christ died for us." When you feel rejected, know that God loves You; so much in fact, Jesus lived, died, and rose again so that we can be with Him—through Jesus we are no longer rejected, but accepted.

Chapter 46

Example

"Follow my example, as I follow the example of Christ."

1 Corinthians 11:1

Leaders, mentors, teachers, role models, each one of these has been influenced in some way by another person. Stop and think about someone you wanted to be like when you were a child, for instance an athlete or actor. Consider who you want to be like now. Is it the same person as before or someone different? What did or did not change? We are impressionable. Some of those impressions are positive, while others are not. Around us are people who follow Christ, the example is Christ. At communion, we remember Christ and the example he set to follow, loving God and people. May others see that we are following the example of Christ; may we be impressed upon and impress other people with Christ's example.

Chapter 47

Strong

"That is why, for Christ's sake, I delight in weaknesses, in insults, in hardships, in persecutions, in difficulties. For when I am weak, then I am strong."

2 CORINTHIANS 12:10

GYMS. WE THINK WE ought to go, we know we should go, we want to go, because we can get stronger. To get stronger, it takes time. It does not happen on one trip to the gym. It takes several trips over the span of months to realize one is strengthening. It is through the arduous sessions that we grow stronger.

Regarding faith, it is through arduous life experiences that our faith grows stronger. It may be unpleasant at the time, but that is what helps us grow, deepen, strengthen. Jesus endured the crucifixion to become the victorious king. Because of Jesus, we are strengthened in our moments of weakness.

Chapter 48

Summed Up

"The entire law is summed up in a single command:
'Love your neighbor as yourself.'"

GALATIANS 5:14

LOVE IS A POWERFUL word. What is love? Why should we love? How hard is it to genuinely love our neighbors as ourselves? How do you treat those around you? How do you respond to those sitting around you here today? These words spoken by Jesus can be traced back to Leviticus 19:18 "Do not seek revenge or bear a grudge against one of your people but love your neighbor as yourself. I am the Lord." God spoke these words to His people. God knows love involves sacrifice. God expresses His love to us and is made perfect by sending His Son, Jesus. Let us remember God's love for us, for humankind, for all people, so that we could have a relationship with Him.

Chapter 49

Now

"But now in Christ Jesus you who once were far away
have been brought near through the blood of Christ."

EPHESIANS 2:13

N-O-W. NOW. WE HAVE become so accustomed to this. We want
service NOW. We eat at a restaurant and want our food NOW. We
do not want to wait; we want it NOW. We associate instant gratifi-
cation with NOW. Not in a few minutes, not half an hour, and not
a year or more later, but NOW.

Thankfully, there is something available NOW—forgiveness
for our disobedience to God, our sins. Forgiveness is available
NOW, not later, not back then, but NOW. Through Jesus death
and resurrection, his blood-shed on the cross, we can NOW experience His forgiveness. Let us be so ever grateful that God's mercy
and grace is available NOW.

Chapter 50

Remember

"I thank my God every time I remember you."

PHILIPPIANS 1:3

REMEMBER IS A POWERFUL sensory-driven word. We remember sounds that we hear and the feelings they invoke. We remember the taste of food and the satisfaction it brings. We remember the touch of something and the sense of protection and warmth. We remember a smell that is invigorating. We remember the sight of something significant. These images or experiences leave an imprint upon us.

A well of emotion erupts when we read or hear these words, "I thank my God every time I remember you." Only a few words describe the impact of these people. At communion, we can echo those same words, "I thank my God every time I remember you," remembering what Jesus endured for humanity.

Chapter 51

Clothe Kindness

"Therefore, as God's chosen people, holy and dearly
loved, clothe yourselves with . . . kindness."

COLOSSIANS 3:12

CLOTHE YOURSELF. WE OFTEN do not think about how difficult it
can be to clothe ourselves. On one hand, I have observed someone struggle to put on a pair of socks. There are times when we
struggle such as when clothes are too small, or we get tangled
up. On the other hand, after much practice, one can easily and
quickly put on clothing.

When it comes to our faith, we struggle with removing 'taint-
ed, sin-stained' clothing. God showed kindness to us by sending
His Son, Jesus, to die on the Cross, so our clothing could be removed and cleansed because of His sacrifice. Because of Jesus, let
us clothe ourselves with kindness.

Chapter 52

All Circumstances

"give thanks in all circumstances, for this is God's
will for you in Christ Jesus."

1 THESSALONIANS 5:18

WHEN IT COMES TO communion, how can we give thanks? On one
hand, Jesus was crucified and laid in tomb. What is thankful for
this? It is what is on the other hand, the tomb is empty. Jesus did
not remain and for this we can give thanks. We give thanks for
his death and resurrection and as we partake of the emblems, we
remember his death and celebrate his victory over death.

Chapter 53

Just

"God is just. He will pay back trouble to
those who trouble you"

2 Thessalonians 1:6

JUSTICE. WHEN IT COMES to lawlessness or unlawfulness, we desire justice. When someone commits a crime, we seek justice. When someone offends, we seek justice. When we disobey God, God is just. God is the Supreme Judge over all, yet when humanity sins, God is just. God can punish for disobedience, however God sent Jesus to this earth to pay the penalty of sin although he did not deserve it. Through Jesus, God demonstrates how just He is, taking the punishment that we deserve upon Himself, so we could be made just before Him.

Chapter 54

Worst

"Here is a trustworthy saying that deserves full acceptance: Christ Jesus came into the world to save sinners—of whom I am the worst."

1 TIMOTHY 1:15

HAVE YOU EVER HAD one of those days where everything seemed to go awry? The more you tried to course correct the further you found yourself out of alignment. No matter how hard you try, it just gets worse. Whether during this or at the end of the day, we may cling to these words to Timothy. No matter the status or condition, Christ came for you and me.

Chapter 55

Remind

"Remember Jesus Christ, raised from the dead,
descended from David. This is my gospel."

2 TIMOTHY 1:8

EVERY ATHLETE NEEDS THE voice of a coach. There are times
when the athlete needs correction for doing something that could
hinder performance. There are also times when the athlete needs
encouragement to do something that improves performance. The
coach corrects and encourages. In a sense, the coach reminds the
athlete. It is appropriate to hear and read these words "remember
Jesus Christ." The writer of this letter encourages Timothy to remember the facts of Jesus, "raised from the dead" and "descended
from David." The words came at the right time and in the right
way. What wonderful timing for us to hear these words at communion, "remember Jesus Christ!"

Chapter 56

Commonality

"To Titus, my true son in our common faith"

TITUS 1:4A

COMMONALITY IS A WAY to determine and distinguish unity. Amid diversity, there can be a unifying element to bond and bridge each diverse aspect. Look at any sports team and see the diverse personalities, skills and positions needed for a team to be complete.

In this letter, Titus was commented as being a part of "common faith." Common faith in what, or who? This common faith is built upon Jesus, a faith built upon the fact Jesus lived, died, and rose again. At communion, we are united in and with Christ. The church past, present and the future, along with Titus, unites to focus upon Jesus as we participate and share the emblems together.

Chapter 57

Active

"I pray that you may be active in sharing your faith,
so that you will have a full understanding of every
good thing we have in Christ."

PHILEMON 6

WHEN I OBSERVE MY daughter, I consider her highly active, especially her active mind. As she plays, she reenacts what she has experienced and observed from singing songs to cooking. As we get older, we become less active, even as Christians. We become regularly active with our faith, but as time passes by, we fall into the trap of thinking we do not need to be active anymore; it is someone else's duty. We are challenged to always be active in sharing our faith. Our faithfulness to Jesus, to his church, to active participation to communion may very well be an extension of sharing our faith as others will notice our priorities and commitment to Jesus.

Chapter 58

Purification

"After he had provided purification for sins, he sat down at the right hand of the Majesty in heaven."

HEBREWS 1:3B

"THE SON IS THE radiance of God's glory and the exact representation of his being, sustaining all things by his powerful word. After he had provided purification for sins, he sat down at the right hand of the Majesty in heaven," states Hebrews 1:3. What more can be said of Jesus? He endured the cross, rose from the grave, and sits at the right hand of God in heaven. At communion, we remember what Jesus did and where Jesus is.

Chapter 59

Pure Joy

"Consider it pure joy, my brothers, whenever you
face trials of many kinds."

JAMES 1:2

HAVE YOU EVER EXPERIENCED pure joy? Not half joy, not almond joy, not a bundle of joy, but pure joy. Yes, these, along with many others, may bring us joy, but is it truly pure joy? It seems that to experience pure joy, one must undergo trials; trials of the body—those that are physically exhausting, mind—those that are mentally fatiguing, and spirit—those that are spiritually grueling. As you may recall, Jesus was exhausted physically, fatigued mentally, and strained spiritually as He approached the Cross. Jesus' death and resurrection ushered in pure joy.

Chapter 60

Steps

"To this you were called, because Christ suffered
for you, leaving you an example that you should
follow in his steps."

1 Peter 2:21

Steps on stairs, steps on sand; step here, step there; watch out
for that step. We take steps in unusual ways in a house, in the snow,
even following the steps of another. Jesus took the steps he was di-
rected by his Father, which led Jesus to the cross then to the tomb;
but the steps did not stop there. As you prepare for communion,
ask yourself are you following in the steps of Jesus?

Chapter 61

Grow

"But grow in the grace and knowledge of our Lord
and Savior Jesus Christ. To him be glory both now
and forever! Amen."

2 Peter 3:18

Growth. We see growth in trees spreading its branches higher
and higher into the sky. We see growth in a child getting faster,
stronger, and smarter. Consider a plant. Once the seed is planted,
it grows to a point to spread more seeds, although it may die.
The life cycle continues; it is ever growing. Because of Jesus'
death and subsequent resurrection, we are every growing in our
relationship with as Lord and Savior. May we spread more seeds
growing in Him.

Chapter 62

Not Only

"He is the atoning sacrifice for our sins, and not only
for ours but also for the sins of the whole world."

1 JOHN 2:2

WE WOULD LIKE TO be selected. It makes us happy. It feels good to
know that you are recognized for something. We appreciate being
acknowledged for something positive and productive. Like an actor
who wins an award or an athlete who is noticed as the MVP amidst
a team, it can be difficult to share the spotlight. Jesus came for all.
Jesus did not come just for me, but for all. We should remember
what Jesus endured and be challenged to share this with others.
Jesus came not for us, but for all throughout the world.

Chapter 63

Walk

"And this is love: that we walk in obedience
to his commands."

2 JOHN 6A

WHEN WE WALK, WE clear our heads, improve our health, carry on a conversation, build a relationship, and on and on. Walking has its benefits. However, walking should be continuous. Jesus walked in obedience to His Father, lived, died, and rose again. Jesus has already paved the way. When we walk according to Him, we walk along the path Jesus has already trotted. A path he has walked on and shown us how to walk as well. Along the way, he walks with us because of his Spirit. Let us walk with Him.

Chapter 64

Imitate

"Dear friend, do not imitate what is evil but what is good. Anyone who does what is good is from God. Anyone who does what is evil has not seen God."

3 JOHN 11

I "COOKED" A SANDWICH according to my daughter and son. It was a peanut butter sandwich. However, I thought it was an opportune time for them to "help cook" a sandwich. We talked about what we needed, especially spending time on the tools needed. Just as they imitate how I make sandwich, Jesus imitated what his Father revealed to him. Jesus shared bread and wine with his disciples and instructed them to do the same. We continue this imitation as we take communion today.

Chapter 65

Keep

"Keep yourselves in God's love as you wait for the mercy
of our Lord Jesus Christ to bring you to eternal life."

JUDE 21

HAVE YOU EVER HAD a favorite? As a child you had a favorite toy.
As a teenager you had a favorite song and still do. Or as an adult
you have a favorite memory. Whatever it is you keep or remember
it because it has significance to you. God shows us his love through
Jesus. He went to great lengths to show us and help us remember
His love because He wants us to remain in him.

Chapter 66

Dwelling

"And I heard a loud voice from the throne saying,
'Now the dwelling of God is with men, and he will
live with them. They will be his people, and God
himself will be with them and be their God.'"

REVELATION 21:3

AT CHRISTMAS, WE ENVISION the baby lying in a manger. At
Christmas, we envision the baby cooing and crying. At Christmas, we envision the baby being cared for by Mary and Joseph. At
Christmas, we must realize the baby's name is Jesus. At Christmas,
we must realize the prophecy is fulfilled when they call him Im-
manuel, which means God with us. At Christmas, we must realize
the baby is born to encounter the cross and to overcome the tomb,
so that we too may dwell with God and be his people.

Appendix A

Instructions

Step 1: Find out the sermon series, typically from a pastor/minister.

Step 2: Find out the sermon text (scriptures) to be used.

Step 3: Pray that your thoughts and writing would reflect Christ.

Step 4: Read the scriptures.

Step 5: Select a key verse.

Step 6: Question 1: What is one word, or phrase, from the Bible that captures your attention?

Step 7: Question 2: How does this word capture the audience's attention?

Step 8: Question 3: How does this scripture, or word, prepare the audience for communion?

Step 9: Write it out with pacing at 100 words per minute.

Step 10: Practice reading the communion thought aloud three or more times.

Appendix B

Sample

Step 1: Stand Alone Sermon

Step 2: Scripture text: John 8:42-47 NIV

Steps 3–5: Complete on your own.

Step 6: Key word: "sent"

Step 7: Sent as in sent a text message

Step 8: How does "sent a text message" prepare
for communion?

Step 9: See sample.

Step 10: Practice reading the communion
meditation aloud.

"Text Alert"

"Jesus said to them, 'If God were your Father, you would love me, for I came from God and now am here. I have not come on my own; but he sent me.'"

JOHN 8:42 NIV

WE LIVE IN A day and age where we are constantly bombarded with pieces of communication flying in at us from cell phone ring tones, e-mail beeps, and text alerts. Some of the pieces of communication we want to hold onto, while others, well we want to avoid. God sent a message. God sent a message to us through Jesus. In a sense, God sent us a text alert, regarding Jesus. Jesus came to live among us, to die, and to be raised to life, where one day, God will send Him once again. Until then, we commune together, recalling these words of Jesus . . . "This is my body, which is for you; do this in remembrance of me . . . This cup is the new covenant in my blood; do this, whenever you drink it, in remembrance of me."